Personal & Business Branding

Go Viral And Make Unlimited Passive Income Building A Loyal Brand Network Through Blogging, SEO, Instagram, Facebook Advertising, YouTube, Email And Affiliate Marketing

Joshua Reach

Table of Contents

Introduction

The Online Entrepreneurial Lifestyle

We can define entrepreneurship as the will and ability to start, run, manage, and organize a new business complete with all its challenges and risks in order to be profitable and earn money out of it. It is said that the most successful entrepreneurs are those that persevere through good and bad times.

An internet or online entrepreneur is an entrepreneur, manager, founder, or owner of a business that is largely or solely based on the internet. Such an entrepreneur earns their money through initiative and by taking certain calculated risks.

Why Start an Internet-Based Business?

There are benefits of starting an online business compared to other businesses that are especially brick-and-mortar-based. You can operate just about any business-type online. This means that you are not limited to small-time gigs such as selling your second-hand items. Some of the largest firms in the world are web-based. They include Amazon, Google, and Facebook.

Online businesses allow you to pursue your dreams and follow your passion. The nature of online business allows you to pursue your passion. This is in contrast to employment where you implement the company's vision and make someone else rich.

Having your own internet based business expands your earning potential. The challenge of working for someone else as an employee is that your earnings are limited to your salary. You will hardly have time to put in extra hours at another job or business. But, as a self-employed individual, you will be able to earn as much as you like depending on your hard work and business model.

You get to choose the hours that you work. The freedom to choose your own working hours means that you can choose to start work early or mid-morning, in the afternoon, or evening and work for as long as you want. This is because the internet is readily available and open for business all the time every single day. Having this kind of freedom is extremely liberating and will improve your quality of life immensely.

You will also save money on costs such as rent and overheads. Ordinary businesses such as brick-and-mortar stores and establishments have to pay a lot of money for rent, overheads, and costs such as salary and so on. On the contrary, most of these costs are eliminated if you work online. You do not need to pay any rent if you work from home. You will also not need employees as you can hire online at much cheaper rates should the need arise.

Build a Loyal Brand and Earn Millions for Many Years to Come

As an online business owner, you need to pay attention to building a strong, loyal brand. Online customers browse the internet in search of products they wish to buy before actually making the purchase. As such, you need to learn the modern ways of building brand loyalty. Here are some tips on how to go about it.

1. Engage your customers

When you connect with your followers, you introduce a feeling of belonging. You should endeavor to share any new developments and exciting news about your brand with your followers. You should also share your opinions so that they are excited and remain engaged. Some of the best platforms to use include popular social networks such as Facebook and Instagram.

2. Be authentic

If you want your customers and followers to trust you and remain loyal, then you should be authentic. This means showing your true self and staying true to your beliefs. Customers will detect anything phony or fake. This will work against you. However, being genuine, honest, decent, and authentic will result in long term trust and customer loyalty.

3. Remain consistent always

After working so hard to define your brand and connect with customers, you will need to remain consistent in what you do. Customers love consistency once they find what they want. Therefore, always refer back to what produced the success and drew customers to your brand. For instance, your messages and logo should be consistent at all times with little or no variation. Also, take the chance to share your values with your audience as often as possible.

4. Understand what makes your customers happy

A lot of businesses fail and brands fare poorly simply because they do not take the time to understand what the customers really want. Customers often abandon a brand when what is offered is different from what they want. Therefore, keep engaging your customers and provide them with opportunities to share their thoughts and opinions. Some businesses offer products that have no space in the market. It is always a great idea to listen to your customers and understand what they want then give it to them.

5. Invest in a professional-looking logo design

If you want brand loyalty, then you should always start with a professional looking logo. This way, if you have good quality products and a powerful brand, then your customers will always identify your brand through your logo. Take time to choose the design and colors carefully so that it exhibits your mood, feeling, and the role that your brand intends to fulfill.

Platforms to Promote Your Brand

There are a number of platforms that you need to use in order to promote your brand successfully. These include the largest social media platforms available today. They include Facebook, Twitter, YouTube, LinkedIn, Pinterest, and Instagram.

We know that almost 80% of adults in the US have social media accounts. Chances are that your customers are also on social media. Promoting your brand on these platforms is, therefore, an excellent way of reaching out to your customers and finding followers who can be converted into customers.

Even as you open accounts and pages for your brand, you should find ways of marketing your personal brand to followers. You should use both paid advertisements as well as options such as word of mouth and organic searches.

Your Personal Brand

If you want to impact your customers and the market greatly, then you need to develop a powerful personal brand. Such a brand connects easily connects a face to a brand or company. This is crucial if customers and the general public are to relate you to your brand.

A powerful personal brand can help you to develop a million-dollar business earning you millions each year easily. You can even develop your personal brand and become a thought leader. This way, people will follow you, buy your books and videos and pay to listen to you speak.

Start from nothing to something

Building your own business does not require much. All that you need in order to get started are a good business idea that addresses a particular problem and passion, energy, and zeal. If you have a burning desire to succeed and your idea solves a specific problem, then you will be on your way to building a successful enterprise.

If you have a hobby, talent or skill, then focus on it and develop it so that it is profitable in the long run. For instance, if you are a great designer with programming skills, then you can create beautiful web content for numerous clients over the internet.

E-commerce and leveraging the internet

If you want to succeed in business today, then you need to learn how to leverage the internet. You should endeavor to learn as much as you can about online entrepreneurship so that you can take advantage of this platform, grow your personal brand, and make huge profits with a great strategy. There are a couple of things you will need to know in order to succeed in your online ventures.

Perseverance

According to some of the most successful online entrepreneurs, the difference between successful online entrepreneurs and failures is perseverance. While it is sometimes tempting and easy to throw in the towel, it is absolutely important that you learn to persevere even when times are hard. Steve Jobs, the founder of Apple Inc., one of the largest and most successful computer companies in the world, once said that the most important trait of a successful business owner is perseverance.

Come up with a suitable business model

You should build a good business model that you can follow and adhere to as you grow and prosper. Such a plan is very similar to a pre-planned flight path that a plane takes in order to arrive at its destination safely. Basically, if there is no business model, then your business may not grow towards success as desired. This is akin to a plane not following a flight path. Such a plane will not arrive at its destination.

Once you establish your business, you should allow it to grow. This means putting in the hard work to build your brand, come up with a marketing plan and implement it across multiple channels. Experience has shown that it is crucial that you allow your business to grow. This means being flexible and letting your chosen business model evolve and expand. This is common especially in today's world of internet-based entrepreneurship.

Your customers will, with time, desire change and a different direction. If your business directs you that way, then you should be willing to make adjustments and accept the changes. In essence, it is crucial to put the interests of your customers first and make any necessary changes in order to remain relevant.

Chapter 1: The Mindset of a Determined Entrepreneur

As an entrepreneur, you probably dream of success and quitting your day job. Maybe you want to earn millions of dollars and live a great life. Statistics show that over 85% of all employees worldwide desire to be doing something else rather than their current jobs.

Even then, quitting your job and setting up a business is just the beginning because there is a lot of work that needs to get done. To establish yourself and your personal brand, you need to put in a lot of long hours and hard work. The first step though should be spent on learning about how to become an entrepreneur. Learning entrepreneurship is often underrated but is the best thing that you can do for yourself if you are to emerge the winner.

Have a Plan and the Right Mindset

Some of the things you will need to do in order to get started include your finances, having a plan, goals, and a well-prepared mind. Basically, your habits will dictate your success. If you maintain the 9 to 5 mindset, then you probably won't fare very well as an entrepreneur. You need to start thinking and acting like other top entrepreneurs who put in the hard work and spend many hours just working hard. In the initial stages, you will really need to work, work, and then work some more. Here are some tips on how to have the right mindset for success as a successful entrepreneur.

1. Train your mind to start thinking out of the box

Once you start your own business, the corporate mentality should exit the door. This means that your working hours will no longer be limited to 8 hours between 9.00 am and 5.00 pm. You will need to, at this stage, open your mind to new and exciting possibilities such as those that never existed as an employee.

If you have a vision and start doing things the unconventional way, people may begin to stop you. They may not understand your vision and desire for success. However, you should not let this stop you. You should be creative and come up with something different and new in order to be successful.

2. Develop both long-term and short-term visions

You should focus on developing a new kind of thinking that focuses on attaining a strategic goal. Basically, you need to have a vision for your brand and company. Have an idea about where you want your business to go and what path you will follow to get there. Being an entrepreneur, it is your vision that will guide your business even if you hire others to help you. The rest of your team will be looking up to you for leadership, guidance, and advice. You should be able to step up to the plate and provide the leadership needed.

3. Take charge and bear responsibility

Back when you were employed, you still got paid even when you had a bad day. In business, you might not get paid when your venture is unsuccessful. On top of not getting paid, there are others counting on you to get paid. While you may probably be able to manage without pay others cannot.

Starting a business sometimes causes an entrepreneur to experience high-stress levels. The stress can get so bad that it becomes a health issue. However, even under such severe stress, you still have to soldier on. You will need to learn to get over situations, muster the courage, and move on.

When you are working to establish your business and create your brand, you will need to motivate yourself. There will be no boss to encourage you and no supervisor around to see that you get the work done. For you to succeed, you will have to stay focused and organized and get used to plenty of hard work and long hours.

4. You will become a jack of all trades

Back when you were employed, you probably had a well-defined role to play. This time it will be different. As an entrepreneur, you will not be able to disown any job as there is no one else to pick up the slack. This will most certainly mean getting your hands dirty and doing work that you are not used to doing. Basically, you need to ensure that everything at your business is running along smoothly. You may need to do lots of tasks including accounting, customer service, IT work, and so much more.

Expect to learn different skills, do lots of menial tasks, and generally work long hours. You should not expect to have it easy at the initial stages. As an entrepreneur, you will not finish work when you get tired but when you are done.

5. Learn to be positive, focused, and flexible

In business, attitude is everything, so you need to always have the right attitude. You should never let any challenges get in the way of your vision. Always remember to be optimistic as every challenge that you meet has a solution. If you do not have the passion for entrepreneurship and building your brand, you may not get very far. As such, giving up is never going to be an option. Instead, have lots of passion in your work and focus on providing the best solution to a problem that a sector of the market has. Therefore, start off with a problem that needs to be solved or perhaps a great idea. Find a solution and do so with passion. This way, you will eventually be successful, and your brand will soar to great heights.

Mindsets that Will Make You a Successful Entrepreneur

One of the first things you need to get off your mind is the idea of getting rich very quickly. While times may be tough and opportunities hard to come by, there is always a chance to overcome the challenges and grow your business. Success and enterprise are often due to some changes and commitments that you make in your life.

Like most successful entrepreneurs, you want freedom in all aspects of your life. You also want to secure yourself and loved ones financially as well as leave them a secure future. You also have a sound product or solution that solves a problem or addresses a particular challenge that exists in society. Your solution should help make people's lives better.

If you can accomplish these feats, then you will become an unstoppable entrepreneur. All you will need to do is make some simple yet crucial adjustments to your life. If you can make these crucial adjustments to your life, then you can expect to see some results sooner or later. Here are a few tips that will help you along the journey.

Do not let expert assistance hold you down

Technology today allows us to receive training, coaching, and advice from anywhere around the world. Advances in technology allow for consultations to take place across vast distances. Therefore, you can consult an expert on a different continent or hire the services of a professional regardless of where they are located. Traveling long distances and spending a lot of money consulting is no longer necessary. These technological advances have provided immense help and opportunities for entrepreneurs, enabling them to take their businesses to the next level.

Even then you will need to be careful because after hiring a coach or consultant, you will start counting on him or her and develop a permission-seeking mindset which is unnecessary for an entrepreneur. There will be numerous times when you will need to make decisions and move forward regardless of all other factors. Therefore, learn to take advice from an expert where necessary but do not become too dependent on their advice. You should learn to be confident in your abilities and capacity to make sound decisions. All that an expert will do therefore is to enhance what you already know or have.

There is no substitute for hard work

It can be tempting sometimes to avoid hard work and put it aside for later. For a long time, you were used to the division of labor as an employee with others around ready to assist you with your chores. However, as an entrepreneur just getting started, you will have to work hard for a long time. This is crucial if you are to grow phenomenally, build your brand, and achieve your goals.

It is human nature to search for shortcuts to obtain quick results. While there are a couple of things that you can do in order to grow fast and obtain desired results, most things require that you put in the hard work and time. There is no substitute for the amount of hard work that it takes to grow and see long term success in business.

Regularly speak powerful words to yourself

Most things that we tell ourselves actually become a reality. As such, you need to speak positive words to yourself regularly. As human beings, when we convince ourselves using words that something is not possible, then it will most likely come to pass. Therefore, learn to tell yourself positive stories. Do this every day or as often as possible and ensure that you fill your mind and soul with positive words and thoughts.

You can say things such as how unstoppable you are and how you can accomplish anything that you set your mind to. Search and find web articles, blogs, videos, and podcasts that educate and motivate you. Also, make sure that you avoid negative individuals with low energy and people who drag you down. It's best to keep away from them because they can influence you negatively and slow you down. Try and obtain a vision of where you want to be and how you want your business to look like. Then keep working towards this vision and do not let anyone try to bring you down.

Avoid the shiny object syndrome

There is a phenomenon known as the Shiny Object Syndrome. This refers to the tendency of a person to abandon their current venture and pursue a new business goal or idea. This is a bad idea, and you should not pursue something new and relatively unknown instead of the business venture that you have planned and invested in for so long.

At its very core, the shiny object syndrome is known as the disease of distraction. This situation often affects entrepreneurs mostly due to their unique characteristics. You will find that entrepreneurs are mostly highly motivated individuals who desire new developments and have a passion for the latest technology. By nature, entrepreneurs do not have a fear of creating new things or starting new projects.

Generally, these characteristics of entrepreneurs are great. They are only troubling when the shiny object syndrome sets in. This situation is very similar to a small child chasing an object. Once they get the object and see what it is, they lose interest and immediately start pursuing something else. When it comes to entrepreneurs, they abandon their current venture and start pursuing new ventures. Avoid this syndrome and remain focused and dedicated to your dream and passion with your current venture.

Work, work, work and then work even harder

Remember that during the initial stages, you will need to put in a lot of hard work. This means working to develop your business. You will need to put in a lot of hard work. As such, you will need to be much disciplined. Do not accept to be waylaid and distracted from your business.

Building your business will be tough especially if you are ambitious and desire to reach the highest levels. You will put in money and lose, you will trust people and they will fail you, and you will generally suffer all manner of setbacks. Despite all these setbacks and challenges, you should persevere and keep on pushing.

A lot of successful entrepreneurs with million dollar empires today also went through similar challenges and suffered for lengthy periods of time. If you stay focused, keep your vision intact, and carry on working as hard as you can, victory will eventually come your way.

Hire a virtual assistant if necessary

Sometimes you may feel overwhelmed or have too much to do. In such cases, you may be unsure of what to do. You should never hesitate to seek help and ask for assistance. If you need help and decide to hire an assistant, then opt for a remote or virtual assistant. A virtual assistant is a much better option compared to a live, walk-in assistant.

A virtual assistant is able to accomplish a lot more because they operate remotely and do not need to spend any time commuting. A live assistant who works from your office is more expensive. Hiring one is also risky because personalities may clash.

Virtual assistants can help with much of your administrative tasks such as replying to emails, data entry, producing content for your social media pages, responding to social media posts and messages, and so much more. This will free you up to attend to more crucial matters such as processing sales and accounts.

There are plenty of places where you can find virtual assistants. These include platforms such as O-Desk, www.virtualassistants.com, Fivver.com, and many others. Once you find a suitable individual and agree on terms, you can proceed to assign them work and then do the rest of the work.

Chapter 2: Personal Branding and Branding for Business

Personal Branding

The term personal branding refers to the process of creating and developing an image or mark around your name and also your career. It also refers to promoting what you stand for and establishing what you believe in. A personal brand includes your unique experiences and skills that make you the unique individual that you are. When done professionally, personal branding will differentiate you from all other experts in your field. When you create a personal brand, you can use it to communicate and express your unique skills, values, and personality.

A brand can be anything

We are used to thinking that a brand can only be related to products or companies. For instance, major brands such as Apple, IBM, or Google are all associated with major companies. Things are a little different nowadays because just about anything can be branded. This includes individuals like you and me because as an individual, you can have a personal brand.

Basically, your personal brand includes what you are mostly known for. If you are a great photographer, an amazing actor, or funny comedian, then that will constitute part of your brand. This brand can exist both online and offline. There are plenty of tools available today that can help you to build and develop your brand. If you intend to create your own personal brand, then you should make use of these tools in order to create an outstanding impression on all those looking you up online.

It is possible for any person, any willing individual to create a brand and harness their power to be unique and stand out. This uniqueness can draw the public to your services and products or help you to get a message out. A personal brand is more about enabling you to present yourself so that the world can get to know who exactly you are and what it is that you have to offer.

Anyone can brand themselves

A personal brand is not something designated only for successful entrepreneurs or established individuals. It should be viewed as something that anyone can have. It will enable you to stand out from the rest. Developing a personal brand provides you with a proactive path of managing your career development and generally how others perceive you in the marketplace.

The very idea of developing a personal brand makes some people uncomfortable. However, you really should put your personal brand out there and take control of your image online. If you do not do this, then you are likely to lose out on numerous opportunities and getting others to control your image and narrative. Therefore, take the initiative and create your own brand and do not let others do it for you.

Personal branding matters

It is never too late to create your own personal brand. Some people might claim that the process is tedious and takes too much time. Others might think it is not worth your time. This is wrong because personal branding, as we have seen, is crucial for your success and presentation both online and offline. Yes, it will take up some time and effort but coming up with a personal brand is absolutely crucial.

People are searching for you over the internet

Regardless of your profession, career, age, it is advisable to create an online profile so people may actually know who you are. Even those seeking employment need a personal brand or an online presence. A prominent human resources organization claims that more than 50% of all employers will not employ anyone without an online presence.

As a fresh graduate or someone at the workplace seeking employment, you will be required to have an online presence or portfolio, and the best format is usually a personal brand. Therefore, take the time to organize and prepare a professional brand that will tell your story and let others know about your skills, talents, experiences, and achievements.

However, as a business person and entrepreneur, a personal brand is even more important. If you seek new opportunities or wish to engage with clients for business purposes, then you will need to have a personal brand. This way, your contacts will be able to see you and check you out if they ever need to just to know more about you.

Personal Branding and the Next Level

One of the most important reasons that should compel you to create a personal brand is to propel yourself forward. Your personal brand will help you take the next step and get ahead. You can consider your personal brand as an added channel for growing and promoting your success. It is an essential step when it comes to working towards achieving your goals.

Creating your brand may sometimes feel like a job

Creating your personal brand may sometimes feel like a daunting task. You may get the feeling that developing your profile is a lot of work. However, this work is essential if you are to have a brand and set it up both offline and online. The crucial part is developing the necessary content needed about your work, your life, and achievements. Once this is done, the rest will be easy and will flow smoothly. You will have established a firm foundation with a clear roadmap making the entire process a lot more manageable. A good personal brand will distinguish you from all the others. You can take control of the branding process by following these simple steps.

Effective Personal Branding Process

We have already established that a personal brand aims to present you as a very marketable, able, and capable brand. A lot of people do get overwhelmed when coming up with material for their brands. However, you should not panic if this happens. Simply take a deep breath and think about your achievements.

Brand building is an ongoing process and not a single event. You can break down the branding process into a number of phases. Even then, this is not a one-time incident and hence the reason why personal branding objectives and process look different for everyone. The process is broken down into three main segments. These pillars are:

- Designing a basic personal brand
- Getting an audience and building credibility
- Begin identifying opportunities

Building your personal brand

You need to first create a personal brand online that showcases your successes, qualifications, achievements, and so on. This way, should anyone search for you online, they will be able to come across a strong profile that showcases your strengths. To achieve this feat, you will need to first do the following:

- Audit your search engine results
- Any unsuitable content not fitting your image should be cleaned up
- Come up with a positive and suitable definition of yourself and brand

- Proceed to create an online presence that basically showcases your achievements, qualifications, and expertise
- Have a personal branding strategy to follow and observe the timelines

The first thing that you need to do before you begin building your brand is to search and find out what is out there. Use major search engines such as Google, Bing, and YouTube to learn what information is out there about you. There are tools that you can use to scan the internet search results for any potentially harmful information.

Should any risky information about you is out there, you should clean it up. You should take any necessary steps to get rid of the negative information. Any that you can delete, un-publish, and get rid of should be removed as soon as possible. You should also search across different websites and social media sites and find out what information is out there about you. Here is what you will need to get rid of:

- Drug use or beer drinking
- Unbecoming behavior
- Poor communication style
- Any polarizing views
- Criminal activity
- Sexual misconduct
- Bullying and violence

After cleaning up all the negative information out there, you will then begin the process of creating your own personal brand. Think about the kind of image that you want people to have of you. For instance, who are you as an individual and what qualities make you unique?

There are other factors that you need to consider. These include your personal branding goals, your professional achievements and ambitions, your audience and how you can build them, things that make you reliable and any evidence that is out there. If need be, you can search for individuals whose personal brands are out there and look similar to what you hope for.

1. Showcase your brand's strengths and achievements

There are ways of showcasing your skills and accomplishments. This is what should follow immediately after you have introduced yourself and presented your persona to the world. Showcase your strengths and achievements by:

- Listing moments when you were recognized your work and achievements
- Putting down the achievements and accomplishments you are proud of
- Think of other private achievements that were recognized

Spend some time and think about all these different situations and then come up with accurate and truthful answers for them all. List them down and make sure they are presentable. Think essentially about what impression you want to leave with anyone searching for you over the internet.

You will need to optimize your personal brand for search engines. If you do not know how to optimize for search engines, consider learning how to do it or hire someone else to do the optimization for you.

2. Build credibility

You will need to build some credibility into your personal brand in order to have placements in third-party websites and channels. After that, you can begin publishing content onto different sites, onto blogs, and all other places. To gain even further credibility, ensure that you post content on high-quality and respected sites.

Ensure that you write content and post it on different credible platforms. You can create different kind of content including blog articles, podcasts, audio clips, images, videos, infographics, and so much more. After posting your content, ensure that you keep track of your publications. Metrics are crucial if you are to keep track of your online performance. Therefore, keep track of all engagements that result from your content on various platforms.

Build an audience

You will need to have an online audience. The first step is to identify who and where your target is. What are the people interested in and what kind of content can I share with them? Once you identify your audience, you should find an influencer among them. This is an outstanding individual who can sway the opinion of your audience and has plenty of influence and say. The influence has the capacity of getting thousands of people to follow you and become the audience that you desire.

When it comes to an audience, you should start with those that you know. This means your friends and family as well as any other followers on your social media sites and email addresses list.

Finally, you will need to engage with your audience and nurture them so that you receive personal branding opportunities. Engage your audience with high quality, relevant, and useful content. Share this content with them and then engage all those who choose to comment, share, or otherwise engage your posts.

If you brand yourself properly, you could earn recognition as a thought leader in your industry. This will, in turn, provide you with numerous opportunities and open doors to possibilities that include interviews, speaking engagements, jobs, partnerships, membership, and a lot more.

Other Things to Enhance Your Personal Brand

Build a platform

Your online personal brand will need to be domiciled somewhere. As such, you are going to need a platform such as a website. Choose your names for your URL address. This will make it easier for others to find you should they search for you. Apart from a website, you will also require social media websites that represent your brand. Therefore, open up personal brand accounts on popular social media networks like Facebook, Twitter, Instagram, and others. Make use of these platforms to share your voice and put your brand out there.

Become a master in your chosen field

Your personal brand will generally paint you as an expert in one field or another. It will also prominently announce your unique strengths, qualifications, experiences, and talent. Learn how to own all these talents and become an expert in your field. Understand that you can never stop learning so keep listening, read a lot and learn as much as you can.

Share your knowledge

Becoming an expert and master in your chosen field is not enough. You need to share your knowledge with others. Therefore, ensure that you teach others, share ideas and showcase your immense wisdom. You can do this with your online audience and on your personal website using videos, podcasts, articles, and so on. Share your knowledge both online and offline.

Be yourself

Remember that you do not need to be anyone else but you. It is your unique personality and individual traits that will attract the kind of audience that you want. Basically, find your own unique style, stick with it, and set a path that others will surely follow.

Set your priorities and identify your values

You will need to then identify your priorities and values. An image of your professional and personal goals in the long and short terms should be clear by now. By doing this, you will be able to identify areas that you need to prioritize and spend more time on. Remember that you will use your priorities and values to guide you in your actions and in the decisions that you make.

Determine your brand persona

Now that you have a clearly defined brand, you will need to come up with a persona. There are a couple of things that you can use to create the persona. These include the following:

- Identify personality features and emotional appeal that you possess
- Describe yourself appropriately
- Clearly define your area of specialization

Make use of the above to come up with your unique persona. Remember that during the initial stages you will have to give and give then give some more before you can start taking. This means to give people ideas, share knowledge, provide useful and informative content and continue doing so until your community, followers, and customers trust you and consider you an expert in your chosen field.

More Things that Will Enhance Your Personal Brand

Even after putting up your personal brand both online and offline, you should take the time to learn a couple of new things. For instance, you should master money online skill. Such a skill will enhance your financial prowess and enable you to keep up with the business world.

Also, focus on building your social media presence. Social media has become a crucial platform for all business owners and renowned personalities. Building a social media following will take a while, but it is something that you can easily do at very little cost to yourself.

Ensure that you are in at least three or four of the major platforms. These include Instagram, YouTube, Facebook, Pinterest, Twitter, and LinkedIn. Doing so will get your personal brand out there with the opportunity to come across billions of social media users. Start a podcast or a YouTube channel and keep it active. Add fresh content regularly. Ensure that you teach those around you. Coach them regularly and help to enhance their success.

You will have to remain alert and watch the performance of your business. Provide free information, tips, advice, and guidance to others, including your followers and general audience. Let them learn to count on you as leader and guru in your chosen field. This way, they will eventually get to trust you and listen to your every word.

At this stage, you will still need to give, give, and then give some more. Keep providing informative blogs and articles, share informative and relevant videos and all other content. It is only after giving so much of yourself and gaining the trust of thousands of followers will you be successful at converting them into paying customers.

Chapter 3: Important Networking Strategies

As you work hard to grow and market your business, you will need to invest in networking. If you are well connected, you will be able to find exactly what you need with just a couple of phone calls. Networking will help to save you time because the right people and resources will always be within easy reach whenever you need them.

Good networking will also bring in clients effortlessly as you will not need to work as hard as others if you apply the best networking strategies. Even then, you can waste a lot of time if you do not network the right way. Business networking is all about being strategic and focusing on your goals.

While most people focus on online networking, you will achieve much better success by meeting people face-to-face. This is because online networking is nowhere near as effective as in-person networking. Here are some effective networking strategies that you can adapt to enhance your business and personal brand

Change your networking strategy

There are plenty of business owners who make plenty of mistakes trying to network as they are often desperately trying to earn an income. Do not focus on how to push your agenda, get all the attention to yourself and possibly manipulate and impress others. Instead think what you can offer others, be helpful and see to their success. Focus on starting and holding friendly conversations and putting others at ease. Basically just think about being sincere, helping others and being generous.

Clearly define your goals

You need to clearly know and understand the reasons why you are networking. People network for numerous reasons. Are you searching for new business connections, new clients, or friends and mentors? Make sure that you closely interact with positive influencers. Also, try and surround yourself with successful individuals who are where you want to be. Ask them lots of questions and learn as much as you can from them.

Previously, business owners and managers focused on networking in order to acquire new clients. This approach never worked out well. However, when the focus changed on finding suitable partners and mentors, then clients came their way. Therefore, focus on finding motivational and inspirational business leaders, influencers, and mentors and the rest will follow.

Get out there and make a great expression

You do not need to waste time. When it comes to networking, you need to get out there and start meeting exciting and amazing individuals. There are always events happening in your town or nearby towns. Find trade shows and networking events that will assist you in achieving your networking goals.

Book events in advance and pay if they charge a fee. Once at the event, have your business cards ready. This is important because you will be able to reach out to others and create a great impression. Make sure that you look your best at these events so that you create a lasting impression. For instance, you can choose your clothes the night before, so they are ready in the morning.

Have your follow up questions ready as well as your elevator pitch. Remember that networking is all about follow-up. Therefore, keep in touch with all the useful contacts that you made. Keep track of all the people in your network and the kind of things you discussed. The difference between meeting your networking goals and missing them depends on follow up.

Essential Networking Strategies

Whether you are an entrepreneur or corporate executive, you will need to develop your networking skills. Networking is crucial because as a small business owner, your clients will consist mostly of referrals from within your network. In fact, referrals often constitute 80% – 90% of all business revenues for small businesses. Here are some skills and strategies you will need to develop if you are to be successful.

Learn to develop a thick skin

You will need to learn how to take "no" for an answer. This will require plenty of patience on your part. If you can be polite and develop a thick skin, then you will fare much better.

Be nice to those you meet

It is important that you learn to be nice to everyone you encounter. This is because you never know when you will need. Sometimes the people you encounter as you build your network or go about your business might come in handy should things get difficult.

Become a great communicator

You should maintain regular interactions with the people in your network or database. You should also work to grow your relationships because most of the time you will be 4 to 5 relationships away from what you want.

One of the best ways of maintaining communication is to meet face-to-face with the people in your database or network. Maintaining consistent and regular contact with individuals within your network is a successful way of communicating. When you are unable to meet in person, then make phone calls or leave personal notes.

Keep it simple

Focus on where most of your resources are being spent especially your energy and time. Think about the kind of results that you want to have. Are you getting these results? Where you see results is where you need to spend your resources. You should not spend your precious time or energy on things that bring no returns.

Gain access to the available resources

Today you can access plenty of resources that can help you with your networking strategies. There are lots of books that you can read. Also build strong relationships with friends, family, and colleagues. Also, join networking groups both online and in person. Make sure that you get connected and stay connected.

Always remember that networking is all about interacting with people, sharing information, nurturing relationships, and expanding your contacts. It helps you build relationships, learning about career opportunities, and so much more. Networking is really a life skill that every entrepreneur should have. It helps to build, maintain, and nurture mutually-beneficial relationships that will last for years to come.

When it comes to networking those who are good at storytelling will emerge winners. Learn how to tell your story and when to tell it. Think about what you want to share and who you want to share it with. People want to hear about your business, about your dream, and about your possible humble beginnings. However, learn how to tell your story, so it is interesting, inspirational, memorable, and entertaining. However, narrate your story in as few words as possible. People may not have all the time to listen to long, unending stories.

Chapter 4: Online Networking Strategies

One of the best ways of presenting your brand to the public and anyone who searches for you to know you better is through a personal blog. If you optimize your blog appropriately using the right keywords and other SEO techniques, then your blog will be really easy to find. Anyone searching for you on the internet using search engines will easily find you.

What is a Blog?

A blog can be defined as a website whose content is produced by an individual. A blog focuses mostly on written content, and the author is often the owner of the blog. Blogs are actually, and the content is known as blog posts. Most of us have probably heard about celebrity blogs and news blogs. However, blogs are not exclusive only to the rich and powerful in society. Anyone can have their own blog.

You can successfully start your own blog and write just about anything that you like. People who write blogs are popularly referred to as bloggers, usually write from a personal perspective. This way, they are able to connect with their readers quite easily. Most blogs also allow readers to leave comments in a comments section. This section appears right after the main blog content. It is advisable to enable your readers to interact with you.

Letting your audience share their opinions and responding to their comments is crucial as it helps to build the connection between the blogger and his or her readers.

In fact, one of the most important aspects of starting a blog is the interaction between the blog owner and his or her readers. This interaction and connection enable you to share information, knowledge, ideas, and matters of general interest with your audience.

Why You Need to Start Your Own Blog

Blogging has very quickly turned out to be among the best ways of spreading news and information as well as communicating. There are essentially millions of blogs across the internet on different subjects, topics, and personalities. Different people from across different nations log onto the internet to find content to read and use. Therefore starting your own blog will open doors for you and enable you to share your profile and any other information that you want.

You should also start a blog because blogging affords you an opportunity to share information with others and to freely express your thoughts and feelings about different issues that are crucial to your or your community. And when you begin writing your blog, you generally become a much better person as well as a better and more improved writer. And the best part about blogging is that you can promote your personal brand, your business, and even make money in the process. Numerous bloggers across America and around the world are earning money from their blogs.

Other Things You Can Do with Your Blog

Earn a passive income: There are other things that you can do with your blog. You can, for instance, make money using your blog. While your income may not compare to some of the top bloggers in the world, you can earn a decent income each week or month. If you learn how to blog and do it the right way, then you will be able to establish a rewarding side gig. A passive income is the desire of numerous people across the globe. Earning an income while doing something else is like a dream come true. For instance, you can spend just a couple of hours per week writing your blog but earn hundreds of dollars within that same week.

Share your story: One of the best ways of presenting yourself to the world and sharing your story is via a blog. It gives you a voice with which to express yourself and your thoughts so that others may get to know more about you. Many writers use blogs to talk about their daily experiences and so much more. This way, they let in others into their lives and also share with others close to them and allowing them to be part of their lives.

Express your personal and business brands: You can use your blog to express your personal brand and your business brands as well. Blogs are extremely effective at this. Apart from your website, a blog is one of the best places online to express your personal brand and put it out there for others to view. If you are seeking recognition among your peers and other professionals in your chosen industry, then a blog is the platform to use.

Identify a suitable community to relate with: We have noted that blogs are inherently interactive platforms. Whenever you post a blog, your followers and viewers will read it and then leave comments at the very end. This provides an excellent platform to interact with others and generally build a community of like-minded individuals with shared interests. You get to teach your followers and share useful information with them. In the end, they will respect you and your opinions and consider you a guru and expert in your field.

Creating Your Own Blog

There are plenty of misconceptions about blogs. For instance, there is a presumption that you have to be a really great writer or trained journalist in order to become a successful blogger. This is not necessarily true because people from walks of life read blogs every day. They do so in search of content that they find suitable and that is of interest to them.

Another thing is that you do not have to write formally at all. In fact, most bloggers are successful because of their casual and informal style of blogging. As an example, people who read blogs about cars do not want to read from an engineer or technician. They would rather read from a fellow motorist with real-life experience.

Have a passion for your topic

To be a successful blogger, there is only one requirement, and that is to have a lot of passion for your chosen niche. Blogging is really all about sharing your thoughts, experiences, ideas, dreams, and hopes. The platform gives you a chance to express yourself and have your content read by thousands and maybe millions of internet users.

You get to choose the topic that you want to write about and then talk about it as passionately as possible. When you do this, you will stand a high chance of success. Essentially, when you choose the kinds of topics that you want to write about, you will succeed because of the passion you have on the topics.

Getting started with your blog

By this point, you are ready to start your own blog. However, where exactly do you begin and what tools or equipment do you require? Here are some basic and easy steps that you can follow.

Questions you need to ask before getting started:

What are you passionate about? This is the most important question to ask yourself. If you have no passion for a topic, then simply do not write, or blog, about it. Passion is an essential ingredient for successful blogging. It will keep you motivated and will prevent you from giving up.

You will be able to develop your skill sets in a particular niche if you are passionate about it. Another reason why passion is important is that if it is lacking, then your readers will pick up on it. And if you do not care, your readers will take off.

Is your preferred niche profitable? It is important to consider the financial benefit your blog could bring. While a lot of people blog because it is something they enjoy doing, it should be profitable as well, for long term sustainability.

Also, consider the fact that it takes quite a while before your blog starts earning you an income. Some of the things you need to keep in mind when you ask this question include your resources, ease of attracting advertisers, whether others are making money in this niche, and what the competition is like. You can use search engines such as Google to find competitors in your niche.

If you want to earn a decent income regularly through your blog, then you need to truly understand whether you can make lots of money in your preferred niche. It is just not worth it spending the next 12 months trying to make money and failing eventually.

Is your niche viable? The truth is that some niches are too small to be viable and growth will eventually climax at a point. From thereon it will be a struggle to increase your traffic, and you will probably run out of content ideas. When considering a niche, you may want to use some keyword tools to get an idea of how many people are searching for a particular keyword.

Some of the keyword research tools that you can use include Google Keyword Planner, Long Tail Pro, and SEM Rush. Even then, the figures you obtain are merely estimates that will guide you in arriving at a decision. Also, look at the competition. If your niche has competition, then it probably is a worthwhile niche. However, if the competition is quite strong and able, then you could run into difficulty because competition may just be too strong.

What does the public really need? It is important that you consider factors such as the importance of your niche to the general public, or specifically, your readers. People have different needs, and according to Maslow's Hierarchy of Needs, there are some needs that are definitely more important than others. For instance, food and water are basic needs which are essential. Video games, on the other hand, are only optional.

Do you need some niche ideas? If you need to get ideas about your blog, then you can find plenty of blogs with ideas. Consider checking out Amazon Best Seller list.
Amazon is one of the most trusted retailers in the world, and this is why simply recommending a product on Amazon can lead to more people purchasing it. The Amazon bestseller list covers all categories that there are. Categories include hot new releases, top rated, and many others.

Choose a name for your blog

Your blog has to have a name. This will be your first task. Therefore, take some time and think about the kind of name that you want for your blog. If you have an idea about what name you'd like for your blog then go ahead and use that name. However, if you really got no idea, then use some resources from the internet to help you come up with a suitable one.

Passion and hobbies: One of the best ways of coming up with a blog name is to work within your hobby or passion. Common passions and hobbies that people have include fashion, cars, sports, travel, and cooking. However, your blog could also be about other less common things such as seafood or Persian culture. There is always an audience for any niche that you choose so follow your passion and you will eventually be successful.

Life experiences: Some people want to write blogs about their own personal experiences. They probably have learned useful lessons which they wish to share with their readers. If you have gone through certain experiences, then sharing this information on your blog will definitely help some of your readers.

Think about some of the extraordinary experiences that you have had. You can write about these and help others with advice.

A personal blog: As a business leader and entrepreneur, you need to have your own personal blog. This is a blog that will showcase your personality, your strengths, achievements, hopes, and future outlook. You can also write about other different topics on your personal blog including a variety of things that you regularly do. Such a platform provides an excellent way of sharing your thoughts with the rest of the world.

Name your blog

It is advisable to choose a descriptive name for your blog. This way, potential readers and visitors from across the web can instantly find out what your blog is all about from its name.

If you intend to write a blog about a particular subject or topic, then ensure that you include this subject within your blog name in some way. Let us assume you want to write about food. You do not necessarily have to include food in the name, but related terms such as recipe, cooking, or meals will do just fine.

For personal blogs, it is best to use your own name because you will probably be writing about lots of different topics. You could also use a variation of your names in a way that will identify the blog as a personal one. There are plenty of different name variations that you could use. Think about all these variations then come up with one that you believe is the most suitable for your blog.

Choose a domain extension

As soon as you decide on your preferred blog name, you will need to choose a domain name. The most preferred in this case is a .com. However, others such as .org and .net are also acceptable. Once you have the complete blog name including extension, you should check and confirm that it is indeed available. If you are fortunate enough and the name is available, then you can go ahead and use it. However, if it is not, then you can try different variations until you find one that is available.

Get your blog online

Now that your blog has both a name and an extension, you need to get it online. This process is not as technical as you may think and can be achieved if you understand what needs to be done. Here is how to go about it.

The first step to getting your blog online requires two things. These are blogging software and a host. The best part is that these often come packaged together. Therefore, identify a good host that is providing suitable and affordable services and have them host your blog. Remember that you must have a blog host if you are to have a blog and get it online. The host will not just provide hosting services but will also provide you with the software that you need to actualize your blog.

There are plenty of web hosts that you can use. A good one will provide you with a number of services including registering your blog name so that no one else uses it. Your host should provide you with free and very simple-to-use software. The most common software is WordPress. This software currently hosts more than 2 million websites and blogs. Once you sign up with one of these hosting sites, the software will be installed and you can then begin working on your blog.

Customize your blog

To get you started, you will need to first log into your account. Use the host's software such as WordPress and log in there. From here you can begin customizing your website, so it looks as neat and beautiful or presentable as you like. There are plenty of options available for you. They range from free to paid profiles to add-ons, images that you can use for your blog, formats, and layouts.

Most blogging software is designed with users in mind. This means that the software is generally easy to use and requires little or no training. You may require a couple of lessons to learn the basics through tutorials. Once you learn these, then you should be able to comfortably use the software and customize your blog as you want. You can find tutorials on YouTube and on the internet should you wish to get further information about how to use the software.

All these changes and options are available to you from the administration page. This page allows you to manage and oversee your blog website the way you want it. Most people have different ideas about how they want their blogs to look. Appearance is apparently very important. This is why the software provided has so many options when it comes to themes, layouts, and so on.

As soon as the theme is installed, you can activate your blog by clicking on the "Activate" blog. It's easy at this stage to view your blog's theme and appearance. Simply enter the URL address into your browser and then take a look. If you want to make a difference, then you can do so through the administration page of your software. Now that your blog is ready, it is time to start writing and publishing content.

Writing and Publishing Blog Posts

Now that your blog is up and running, you need to start writing content and publishing it. This is easy to do. When you log onto your blog, you will find a default blog there. This is okay, and you can always delete it. You can now proceed to write your very first blog. You can do so directly on the site or offsite on a word processor such as MS Word then transfer and publish it on your blog.

Remember that you are free to write just about anything that you like, especially if yours is a personal blog. However, if it is a topical blog where you write content within a specific niche, then focus on matters within that industry. If you are happy with your post, then feel free to publish it as soon as you are ready. If there are any changes that need to be made, then make those changes before publishing the post.

You may realize after publishing your post that it does not look appealing on its own and would look much better with a photo or image. If you want to add an image, you will first need to ensure that you find a suitable one which does not violate any copyright laws. Once your image is ready, you simply need to publish it using the button provided. Now that you have your content ready, take a look at it and rectify any errors or mistakes. If it is perfect according to you, then it is ready for publishing.

Choosing blogging topics

As a blogger, you will often be advised to blog about a topic or niche you are passionate about. While there is some truth to this statement, the best advice would be to tell you about the best niches you should consider. This is if you really want a large audience, be influential, and earn a lot of money.

If you are to be a successful blogger, then you should think about blogging with a purpose. This increases your market share, revenue growth, consumer engagement, and of course, a return on your investment. Blogging with a purpose applies whether you operate a business or not. The aim here is to be a successful blogger.

Problem choosing niches

There is a problem that many bloggers face and this is choosing the wrong niche for your blog. There are a number of reasons why a particular niche could be wrong for you.

Passion: It could be that you are not passionate enough about a particular niche or topic. Perhaps you do not understand it well enough, or it could be a difficult one. Plenty of people have spent a lot of money and time blogging the wrong niche only to realize this about a year or so later.

Money: Some bloggers set out to simply make money. Such a blogger picks on a niche they believe will make them a lot of money. A couple of months or years later, they realize they have no zeal or passion for the niche, and so they begin losing followers. Basically, when your heart is not into something, your audience will realize, and they will start leaving in droves.

You also could be passionate about a niche, but then blogging does not make you any money. While having passion is great, making money is equally important. The financial strain that may result when you don't make any money could lead to serious challenges, and you may eventually be forced to quit blogging.

As a blogger, you need sufficient passion and drive to keep going. You also need to be able to earn plenty of money from your blog to provide you with the financial freedom that you always wanted. There are a good number of people who are earning six-figure incomes annually merely from blogging. There is no reason why this should not be you.

Chances are that the decision of which niche to blog about could affect the next five to ten years of your life especially if you are in it for the long haul. To be successful, you have to take every little factor into account.

Publishing the Blog

Now that you are ready to showcase your blog and share your post with the world, all you need to do is to publish the blog. First, click the "publish" button then go to your software page and take a look. Find the "Launch" button so that your blog is launched officially on the web. When this happens, then your blog will be published on the internet and will be available to anyone who wants to read your posts. Congratulations! Your blog is now live!

Promote the Blog

Now that your beautifully designed website with excellent content has been published you need to promote it so that people get to know about it. You should keep in mind that writing and publishing a website as well as creating and designing a blog are just the initial steps. Without promoting the blog and letting others know about will mean that all your work was in vain.

There are millions of published websites that are published but are never viewed or read by anyone. This is because people are unaware about the existence of the blog. You will have to promote your blog and let everyone get to find out about its existence. This means taking proactive steps to advertise the blog and letting as many people as possible know about your website and what they can expect to find.

Promote your blog on social media

One of the best ways of promoting your website is to use your social media accounts. If you have an account or presence on the popular social media websites such as Facebook, Twitter, Instagram, and so on, then you can use these to promote the blog. First, you should post your blog's link onto your social media pages, so interested followers and friends can follow the link and read your blog.

One of the benefits of using your social media accounts is that there are plenty of people you know on these sites. Most of these people are probably your friends or following you. Share the link with them and let them learn about your blog's existence. These friends and followers are likely to share your link with others so that there is a multiplier effect. This means that more and more people will view your blog and read your posts. If you do create high-quality blogs, then you have a high chance of attracting a huge audience within a short period of time.

Another form of promotion that you will need to work on is to retain your readers. Basically, you will want all your readers to come back after reading your initial post. As such, you will need to maintain contact with these visitors. The best way to do this is to collect email addresses. This is easy to do because you can collect email addresses of your readers.

Email marketing

There is a tool that you can install on your blog to politely request email addresses of your visitors. Use this email tool to collect and create a list of interested followers and readers. Once you have a list of emails, then you can use them for email marketing. This means sending regular email messages to your followers whenever you publish a blog. Your followers will be happy to receive updates and notices whenever something new is published. This is way more important than you might think, so make sure you build your email list. Realize that no one can take this from you and it's another way to market to your customers.

Since you will keep in contact with your followers via email and blog, you will be able to develop a closer relationship with them. When you develop a closer relationship with your followers, they will trust in you, and they can easily become your customers should you create a business.

Comment on other blogs

Another way of advertising and promoting your blog is to read other blogs and leave comments on the posts. When you comment on these posts, leave behind comments and provide useful information and feedback. Try and paint yourself as an expert on the subject matter then guide other readers to your blog by including a link back to your blog or to a specific post.

Other readers on these other blogs will see your comments and will likely follow the link back to your website. Please keep in mind that this is a great opportunity for you to put your blog right in the face of numerous other readers. Make sure that you are polite and very professional and you will attract a lot of additional viewers.

It is advisable to focus on popular blogs with hundreds of thousands of readers and followers. These include platforms such as Quora and others. These sites receive millions of visitors each day. You can tap into this viewership and attract as many of these viewers as possible. This way, you will enjoy additional visitors to your blog.

Guest posting

Yet another way of popularizing your blog is through posting content on other blogs and websites as a guest. There are numerous places all over the internet where you can post your content and share it there. Many websites invite guests to post on their blogs so take the time to contact the owners of these blogs and ask to post. This happens all the time so you will have numerous opportunities. However, not all bloggers welcome guests to post on their blogs. Therefore, make sure that you contact willing blog owners and then proceed to create high-quality content on their blogs. Make sure that you also include links that lead back to your website. If people love your writing and enjoy your content, then they will definitely visit your website and will become avid followers. This is yet another way of providing you with new followers and readers. You can then collect their contacts and email address for your mailing list.

Monetize your Blog

Did you know that you can make money through your blog? Apparently, a blog provides you with an excellent opportunity to make money on a regular basis. This kind of income is known as passive income because you only work a few hours each week while earning money regular from your venture. It is important to understand that there are various ways of making money and earn a profit through activities on your blog.

There are things that can earn you a profit. These include providing services and selling products to your clients and generally selling to the general public. If you have a good product or a quality service, then you can sell it and make a profit. However, there is an even easier way of making money from your blog, and this is through the sale of advertising space. By selling advertising space, you will make money on a regular basis this way.

If your readership increases with more people reading your posts, then numerous advertisers will seek you out and offer you money for advertising space. One of the best providers of advertising opportunities is Google AdSense. Google will find advertisers for you and sell space on your behalf. Therefore, seek out Google AdSense and place the code on your blog. Once you do this, you will not need to struggle with finding advertisers because Google will do all the hard work on your behalf.

Monetize your blog through affiliate programs

If you want to make money through blogging, then one of the best ways to do this is through affiliate marketing. There are plenty of affiliate marketing programs available. As an affiliate marketer, your job will be to first attract interested persons to your website through the content that you produce and then redirect these visitors onto a third party website to a particular product and service. If they purchase the product or pay for a service, then you will receive a commission.

The process is really simple. First, you need to find a suitable affiliate program. Not all programs out there are suitable for find one that is. One of the best affiliate programs is offered by Amazon and is known as Amazon Affiliates.

You can also consider affiliate aggregator services. There are firms out there that actually provide aggregation services to blogs like yours if you write on a diverse range of topics. In general, you will need to come up with high-quality content that actually sells. This is not hard to do if you are passionate about your niche. Take your time to research information and then present in a manner that everyone can read and understand. Use affiliate advertising only as an additional resource.

Remember to maintain a reader-friendly environment within your blog. Your readers come to your blog primarily to read your blogs and possibly leave comments. Keep it that way for the most part. It is important that you maintain a balance between actual blogging and monetization. User experience must be kept high otherwise your readers may be bombarded with marketing messages and disappear.

SEO: Search Engine Optimization for your Blog and Website

The term SEO stands for search engine optimization, and it refers to all the activities necessary to optimize your website or blog for search engines. When you have a blog or website, you want anybody searching for you using search engines to be able to find you. If you do not optimize your blog, then no one will probably ever come across it, and it may as well not exist.

In fact, any person with a blog or website should optimize it, or it does not exist. Apparently, over 80% of web users start their internet browsing on search engines. You want them to find your blog if they are searching for content or information relevant to your industry. Basically, SEO will help you get the reach that you want. If you wish to reach out to a large following, then focus on the keywords that will enable you to do that.

Since you have a blog, you need to know that content writing is crucial for every SEO strategy. You need to develop high-quality content for your readers on a regular topic. If you do this, then you will be enhancing your chances of getting found by internet users searching within your industry.

Keywords

Your content should also contain the necessary keywords. According to experts, your optimization process should begin with keyword research. It is crucial that you figure out the most important keywords that you should use with each post. Learning how to do keyword research is essential because you need to identify the correct keywords for your post. Use the keywords that you want to rank for. For instance, if you are writing about exotic birds, then use keywords affiliated with exotic birds. These could include tropical parrots, African owls, and so on.

On-page SEO

There are a couple of techniques that you can apply to your blog page. These are the on-page techniques that you need to focus on. The first is the URL link. You need to optimize this link appropriately. Use the topic of your post as part of the URL. This way, you will not only optimize the page but will make it easier for anyone to know what your page is all about. For instance, if your blog is about exotic birds and you are writing a post about "Tropical birds in Mauritius," then your URL would look something like www.exoticbirds.com/tropical-birds-in-Mauritius.

You should also maintain the correct keyword density. The best ratio for optimum keyword density is 2%. If you use fewer keywords, your search engine ranking will be lower, but if you use too many, then you will be penalized by the search engines for keyword stuffing. Therefore, be careful with your keywords. If you get it right then, your blog will rank highly, but if not, your rankings will be affected.

You need to learn where to place keywords. As an SEO expert, you should use your keywords on the heading, the title, the first line of your post and the last line. Sometimes it is advisable to use the keyword somewhere in the body of your post. In many cases, bloggers use more than one keyword. In such cases, then you should designate one of them as the main keyword. The rest will be additional or other keywords. Remember to observe the 2% keyword density rule for posts, not more than 500 words.

Other SEO formatting requirements

To improve your SEO, you will need to do additional optimization. These include formatting your images for SEO. Images have titles so optimize these titles. If there are any related links, then optimize these as well.

You need to make use of Meta tags. A Meta tag is a generated HTML tag that enables search engines to recognize the description, title, and additional information about a URL. These do have a slight impact on keywords, therefore, make use of them.

Also crucial to have are Meta descriptions. This is a brief description of a blog or website that described briefly what the blog is all about. It is often not more than three lines long and appears after a search is conducted.

Comment section

Your blog will most likely have a comment section where readers are free to leave comments based on the post they just read. There are readers who like to leave comments together with an external link. This is ok as it is allowed. However, you need to block search engines from crawling through that particular link.

You should also format the comments section. You need to moderate this section to prevent spam comments and things like that. When replying to comments from your readers try and make use of your keywords as well. This will help boost your ranking as well.

Finally, remember that the bottom line and the most important part of your blog is the post. This means that the content needs to be top quality without any compromise. Your readers and all other visitors to your blog will appreciate quality content that is beautifully written, interesting to read, and informative. SEO should not distract you from the readability of your post. If you follow these basic tips, you will end up with a high-quality blog post that is aptly optimized for search engines, making it easy for web users to find and read.

Chapter 5: Social Media Marketing and Advertising

Introduction to Social Media Marketing

The term social media is a general term that refers to totally different websites that provide platforms for social actions. For instance, Facebook is a website and social network that enables users to share photos, updates, videos, stories, links and so much more. On the other hand, Twitter is yet another social network even though it is drastically different from Facebook. It essentially allows users to share short snippets, links, and updates.

Social media marketing provides a powerful avenue for businesses of all sizes to access and address customers and prospects. Most customers are on social media already and are interacting with lots of other brands. Therefore, if you are not reaching out to them via social media, then you are losing out big time. Using social media for marketing purposes is bound to bring you remarkable success. You will be able to create an amazing and respected brand and even drive sales and leads.

Getting Started with Marketing

You do not need to be a rocket scientist to be a successful marketer. However, you do need a sound strategy if you are to be successful in your campaigns. There is no single marketing solution for all businesses. Each small business is different from all others. Therefore, you need to come up with a marketing strategy that is best suited for your business.

The nature of your business really does not matter. This is because all businesses need to have a marketing strategy. Therefore, whether you have a consulting business, a café, an auto garage, a grocery store, or a consignment shop, you will need to find ways to bring in customers to your business. If you are to be successful in your endeavors, then you need to understand the process of deciding on a plan, sticking with the plan, and applying the same resources and time needed.

The marketing process

1. Get the know-how: The very first thing that you need to do is acquire the know-how regarding marketing. As a business owner, you really need to know exactly what to do because marketing can be a tricky path to navigate. Having the skills and knowledge on how to conduct a successful marketing campaign is crucial. Therefore, take the time to acquire marketing skills that will enable you to market your business and products effectively.

2. Set goals and plan a budget: Now that you have the necessary knowledge that you need to define your end goal then come up with a suitable budget. You really need to know exactly what you want. For instance, if you sell products, you will want these products to get to a certain niche in the market. When customers buy your products, you will make a profit. Therefore, think about what is important to your business and how far you want to extend your reach. Remember to prioritize your goals by defining your most crucial needs and your long-term endeavors.

Marketing is also a numbers game. You need to set attainable goals and have ways of measuring your success. You also need to ensure that you only engage in efforts that will directly or indirectly bring results. Efforts that do not bring in new business are of no use to you. Therefore, have well-defined goals in terms of profit, revenue, costs, new sales and number of inquiries. These will help you to keep a tab on your marketing efforts.

3. Identify your target market: One of the most important steps you will need to make is to identify who your target market is. Apparently, not anyone who is walking and talking is your target market. To determine the demographic that constitutes your market, you need to do a few things including market research and conducting surveys. The data you receive from these processes will then be analyzed, and the information will point you in the right direction. You will be able to determine who your target market is and in what niche they are in. It will then be possible to craft or design a marketing campaign around your market niche and target audience.

4. Marketing is more than just advertising: There are numerous aspects to marketing and not just posting adverts or creating websites. If you own a small business, you will have numerous ways of marketing your business beyond advertising. It will benefit you greatly if you find out which marketing tactics work and which ones are not suitable for your niche. Eliminate the ones that do not work so you do not waste any unnecessary funds, time, and effort on them.

5. Put your customers first: You need to take time and really get to know who your customers are. When you get to understand them and know what it is that they really value and want, then you will be well on your way towards a successful marketing campaign. Even after you get new customers, you need to keep in touch with them after the sales and let them understand that you are concerned about their welfare. Try and ensure that you stay ahead of the competition by putting your customers' needs first.

6. You have to spend in order to earn: As a marketer and entrepreneur, you need to understand the principle that you have to spend in order to earn. Basically, nothing comes out of nothing. In order to gain customers and make sales, you will need to spend some money. Marketing is a huge task, and you will need sufficient funds in order to finance these tasks. However, you will reap profits out of your efforts if you spend money where necessary.

7. Make use of social media: A lot of consumers today are on one social media or another. Social media has become so popular that people use it almost on a daily basis for different purposes. Some seek information while others look to share information and news items. Many others wish to find entertainment and anything of interest. Learn how to make use of social media and make sure that it becomes a major aspect of your marketing campaigns.

How Social Media Marketing Helps with Marketing Goals

The best part about social media is that it can be your business' best friend. You can use it adequately to achieve a couple of goals. These goals include some of the following:

- Increasing brand awareness
- Building and enhancing conversions
- Increasing web traffic
- Creating a positive brand association and identity
- Enhancing interaction and communication with an audience

Basically, the larger and more engaged your social media audience is, the easier things will be for you. This will ensure that you achieve most of all your marketing goals. There are numerous social media websites out there. You can use one or more of these websites for effective marketing campaigns. We will now examine some of the more popular social media sites one at a time.

Facebook Advertising

Facebook is the world's largest and most widely used social networking websites. Statistics show that there are more than 2.2 billion users around the world using this popular social site. This massive global audience means that Facebook is a powerful marketing platform for just about all businesses.

If you are a small business owner, an aspiring entrepreneur, or any other enterprise, then you should take advantage of the massive opportunities provided on this social media platform to market their services or brands and leverage this powerful resource for massive profitability.

Paid advertising on Facebook

There are many different ways of reaching out to consumers on Facebook. One of these is by simply opening a page or creating a profile. You can then invite friends and others that you know, so they join you and follow you. After that, you can share content and leverage or harness the power of Facebook to invite more followers.

Posts and powerful content are other examples of Facebook marketing techniques. You can share content of all kind with your followers and then ask your social media followers and friends to share your content. If you have a brand and products or a service to offer, you can post images and share content and links about this service and let others know.

All these are effective solutions for Facebook. However, they will not get you very far because your reach is limited. Fortunately, we have Facebook ads. Paid advertising on this platform provides one of the most trusted ways of reaching out to followers and interested persons within a niche or industry. You can pay for Facebook ads and use them to achieve certain aims. These could be increasing your reach, advertising your brand, or even searching for customers.

Targeted Facebook ads

Facebook has certain powerful features that make ads very effective. Micro-targeting is one such feature. Using micro-targeting, you can reach out to numerous users all at the same time. If you wish to reach, for instance, American males between ages 25 – 45 living in Madison, Wisconsin, then Facebook can help you attain this kind of reach.

Facebook ads enable you to reach your desired target audience according to interests, location, demographics, and sometimes even behavior. Basically, you are able to reach out to the exact kind of people you think are most receptive to your business, message, brand, and products. A lot of people are making money out of Facebook ads.

Targeted ads are beneficial because they enable you to reach out your preferred audience at very low prices. Traditional ads are very expensive and are never targeted at a specific or desirable group. As such, these ads are great for conversion rates, excellent for your budget, and you get a good return of investment.

Facebook ads actually charge you to reach out only to your most valuable followers and most potential customers. However, there is not one type of advertisement only but several. It is crucial to understand all about Facebook ads and exactly how they work. There is an entire process involved ranging from planning your very fast ad to more advanced techniques and advertising strategies.

Facebook is definitely the platform where your business should be. This is because of the numerous users as well as the great business opportunities the platform affords you. However, many other businesses are also on Facebook battling for the same opportunities. Facebook organic reach has been declining in the past couple of years, so a proper strategy, in this case, is necessary. Here are some tips on how to skyrocket your traffic reach.

Use content that is optimized to generate shares and attract attention

For successful social media experience and increased reach, you should consider using highly sharable content. Such content is the kind that causes users scrolling down the timeline to pause and read your post. Such posts should be so inspiring that readers feel a strong need to share with their followers. You will be rewarded handsomely for your engaging content by Facebook.

Try and post less content

A lot of time, Facebook users believe that more is better. However, people do not like being overwhelmed with content and posts on the timeline. It is crucial to understand the importance of tidbit information. There are those who believe you must post over 30 times each month and share over 5000 links in order to get ahead. In reality, less is more, and it is better. Post fewer items but ensure the ones that you do post are of excellent quality.

Increase engagement by boosting your best posts

If you wish to get more traffic from Facebook, then you really need to reach more of your followers. One of the ways of doing this is by boosting your best posts. For starters, you have to produce top-notch content. This is necessary if you are to see any major results. You should expect your traffic to skyrocket if you can create engaging content that is of high quality.

Combine Facebook ads with email and target repeat visitors

If you wish to drive Facebook traffic to your website, then you can use this indirect method for success. You will need to have the right audience for this. Basically, you will first provide a simple way for Facebook users to join your email list. The button to join the mailing list is very visible, and the process takes only a few seconds.

Give audience engagement priority

As a business owner, you should seize every opportunity that you get to engage your audience. The reason is that personal engagement is what keeps them coming back. You need to maintain polite, casual engagement and then share or like their posts. When your followers or other Facebook users leave a comment, this is a way of engaging you in conversation. Make sure to respond to their comment and keep the engagement going. When your audience feels that they are being heard and their opinions matter, they will engage you even further and will become loyal followers and possibly customers.

Different types of Facebook ads

1. Photo ads

One of the best ways of getting started is through photo advertisements. They are easy to design and post and take a very short while to prepare. You are able to come up with a photo ad and use it for various purposes such as to boost an existing post on your page. Photo ads are fairly simple by nature, but they are hardly boring.

2. Video ads

Video ads are among the most powerful ads on Facebook. They are able to showcase things in action. This is crucial because the power of vision, especially with motion, is much more powerful compared to posts and articles. The video can be powerful even without any audio. However, a video with sound is extremely powerful.

3. Carousel ads

Facebook also provides carousel ads. These are ads that use a series of photos and sometimes videos to market your services or products. Carousel ads are great at highlighting different aspects of a product or even a number of different products. You can also use carousel ads to come up with a big image that sends a powerful yet interesting image.

Other types

Other types of Facebook ads include slideshow ads and collection ads. Slideshow ads are self-explanatory while collection ads are designed specifically for use on mobile devices. Collection ads work together with other applications to enable Facebook users to buy products directly on Facebook without leaving the platform.

Learn how to set up a Facebook ad

1. Begin by setting up goals for your ads

The first step you need to take before placing an ad on Facebook is to determine the reason for the advertisement. You need to have a really good reason for placing Facebook ads. When you set out your goals you will be able to come up with more effective ads. You will also be in a position to measure the effectiveness of your ads because there was a purpose for the ads in the first place.

As an example, let us assume that you desire to have more people download your app onto their phones. In this case, you could have a goal of about 100 downloads per month. This way, when you place an ad, you will be able to measure its effectiveness after the one month period comes to an end. Here are other aims and ambitions that you may have when it comes to Facebook ads.

- Generate new leads
- Boost engagement for our Facebook Page
- Increase the number of attendees to an event
- Boost your Facebook Page engagements
- Increase traffic from Facebook to your website

2. Get to Facebook Ads Manager

Once you have determined the purpose for your Facebook ads, you should then head to Facebook ads manager tool. This is the program that runs and manages all of Facebook's ads. When you visit your Facebook page, check out the "Manage Ads" button and then choose the ads manager from here.

From here, you should navigate to the menu and take a look at the options available to you.

3. Determine your objective with the ad

Once you have your ad ready, you should then indicate what your objective with the ad is. This is important because you are placing the ad hoping to achieve a certain objective. Basically, you will have about 15 different objectives for your campaigns to choose from. These can be categorized into three main ones including conversions, considerations, and creating awareness.

Awareness: When you use Facebook ads to create awareness, then you can hope to achieve some of the following objectives.

- Promote your page
- Boost your posts
- Increase brand awareness
- Reach out to people close to your business
- Extend your reach

If you have a small budget, then you are likely to benefit the most based on the awareness that such ads can create. For instance, at the cost of just $1 each day, you can increase your reach by over 4,000 persons.

Consideration: When it comes to consideration, then some of your objectives are those that actually get your viewers thinking about your establishment and then start learning more about you, the brand, and your products. They include:

- You can redirect followers to a location on Facebook or off
- Increase number of people attending your events
- Have users download and install your app
- Collect business leads
- Have people view your videos

Conversions: As a Facebook user, you may want to buy ads in order to persuade customers to purchase products or pay for services at your store. The store could be online or even a brick and mortar establishment. When it comes to conversions, you could also have the objective of

- Maximize engagement on your app
- Have more engagements on your website
- Promote a catalog or your brand and products
- Have people take up on your offer
- Have customers grace your shop

Once your objective is determined, then you should proceed to name your campaign. Getting more followers on Facebook is desirable for every business and all entrepreneurs. Here are some ways that you can get started on Facebook in order to promote your brand and increase visitor numbers.

4. Determine your budget and audience

You need to determine who your target audience is as far as your business is concerned. This is absolutely crucial if your Facebook ads are to be successful. There are a couple of demographics that determine your audience. These demographics include age, languages, location, gender, behaviors, interests, and connections.

If you can, make sure that you also select advanced settings for better or more accurate targeting. Advanced targeting lets you exclude or include those affiliated with certain apps, pages, or events. You are also able to target people that already bought products or paid for services on your website. This is known as retargeting.

Set your budget

Now that you have determined all the necessary metrics for your ad campaigns, the next step is to determine your budget. You should determine how much money you need to spend on your ads.

Facebook offers you a couple of options. For instance, do you want to pay a daily fee or a lifetime fee? You need to keep in mind that the fee you indicate is the maximum that you are going to pay or intend to pay. If not, then you will get to choose between a lifetime budget and a daily budget. The daily budget is the total amount that you pay each day while a lifetime budget is the maximum amount that you will spend in the lifetime of the ad.

Getting started

Getting started on Facebook is easy. However, you need to be cautious in order to get it right. The first step is to come up with a Facebook marketing plan. This plan will list your objectives and then mention the different ways you will use Facebook to achieve these objectives. Objectives could be to promote your brand, gain more followers, convert leads, retain current customers, and so on.

Once your strategy is in place, you should proceed to open a Facebook business page. Your business profile on this popular social media is really a huge part of your online identity. Therefore, take time to create a professional page that is presentable and with all the relevant contact information. Remember it is from here that you will engage your contacts and followers.

As soon as your page is up and running, you should begin posting content and sharing it with others. There are numerous kinds of content that can be posted on this social media. They include videos, links, posts, memes, photos, stories, and so on. Remember to keep the content fresh, entertaining, and interesting.

Tips and advice on Facebook advertising

As a Facebook account holder and entrepreneur, you should learn a few tips about how to create effective ads targeted at your preferred audience. Here are some tips that you can apply.

1. Experiment with audience targeting

Before investing fully in an ad, first try and target a narrow audience and then see how it goes. If your targeting is accurate, then proceed to broaden it. You can broaden your targeting by adding categories one at a time. You could, for instance, start with a broader category of people within a certain region and then narrow this down more and more until you can accurately get down to an exact niche. This makes it easier for you to be able to understand how to narrow down your target audience and how this affects results.

Using this approach, you will also be able to come up with a variety of ads for different groups depending on your needs on different occasions. For instance, you can have some customers who buy during special occasions and others who are more regular customers. Also, you can come up with ads for first-time customers as compared to ads for existing customers. At other times you may want to have promotions or events targeted at a different audience altogether.

You will need to be careful, though, with the kind of assumptions that you make regarding your audience especially during the selection of your options. For instance, some advertisers use just one language when targeting their customers in Europe even though Europeans in different countries speak different languages.

2. Make use of Facebook pixel

If you want to have more effective ads, then you should make use of Facebook pixel. This is a tool that can support your ads if placed on your website. Pixel will do a couple of things for you including creating lookalike audiences, remarket to audiences that have checked out products or services on your website and also track conversions.

Sometimes you may not be able to make use of all the advanced strategies that you are able to implement using this tool. However, just having this tool on your website is advisable. This way you will also be able to track the performance of your ads and then use any data collected to adjust your marketing message.

3. Make use of the best videos and photos

There are some things that Facebook users just cannot stand. These include unclear images, pixilated or blurry photos, and poor-quality videos. While your words are important and texts are crucial, nothing is more powerful than an image. The visuals that you use need to be top notch, high quality, interesting, informative, and able to impact viewers. If you are selling a product through Facebook, then you should follow Facebook's direction and use photos showing people using your product and how they are benefiting from it. This is more effective than just having an image of the product.

4. Make sure that you test everything

As you use Facebook ads for your business, you should not make any assumptions regarding what to expect. Instead, you should test anything that you are trying out for the first time. Test anything new against something that you tried in the past. This way, you will be able to notice if there were any improvement and benefit based on metrics that you consider important to you.

5. Keep track of performance then optimize

When you place ads on Facebook, it is crucial that you keep a tab on them. When you watch the performance of your ads, you will be able to note what is working and what is not. Any campaign that is generally not performing satisfactorily or as expected, you can withdraw any funds allocated to its budget and reallocate the funds to another fund that is performing as expected.

Basically, if you are placing your first ad on Facebook, then it is advisable to place more than one advert. Since the ads are quite affordable, this will not set you back at all. Placing a number of ads will help you find out which ads are working and which approach is best for your clients. You can only identify a winning campaign after placing a couple of ads and determining the most effective of them all.

Instagram Marketing

Instagram

The social network website Instagram is unlike other social media platforms. Apparently, over 70% of its members live in countries other than the US. Most users also happen to be millennials who range in age from 16 to 24 years. Therefore, if you own a business that targets millennials, then this is the best site for your marketing and advertising campaigns.

There are more females than males on the site, so it is great if you are selling to women. Instagram is also highly recommended for businesses with an international audience. The site is also popular with men even though women are slightly more. Therefore, you can equally target men as much as women. Most users access Instagram from a mobile device so try and optimize your posts and promotional messages towards a mobile platform.

Instagram describes itself as a platform that provides you with an exciting and fun way of sharing your experiences with family and friends through photos, images, and videos.

Instagram is one of the largest social media websites. According to statistics, there are over 5 million businesses that use Instagram to connect with their customers and followers, tell their stories and promote their brands. The website receives a cool 1 billion users each month as of July 2018. This makes Instagram one of the largest and most important social networking websites for both individuals and businesses.

Getting started with Instagram is not at all difficult or challenging. Virtually anyone can open an account and start sharing posts or commenting on content on the website.

Tell your story on Instagram

Instagram is a platform where users share their stories and lifestyles. You do this by sharing mostly photos, images, and videos. Only on rare occasions do users share links or written content. If you live a great life that others envy and admire, you can share pictures of your home, car, office, and your excursions to the store, mall, and so on. Post these on your Instagram page for your follows to see and comment on.

Setting up your Instagram account and profile

The first step that you need to take is to visit the Instagram website or download the app if you are using a handheld device such as a smartphone. You can download the app from Microsoft Store, Google Play Store, or the App Store. Once downloaded, you will clearly see the "Create Profile" button. Click on this button to begin the process of creating your Instagram profile.

Profile photo

You will need to provide a photo to go with your profile. If you are opening a personal account, then you should choose a photo of yourself. However, you can choose a different photo for a business account such as your logo. A logo is great for your business, so you get to advertise or promote your business from the word go.

Once your photo is approved, the next requirement is your profile information. You need to provide both basic as well as detailed information about yourself or your business. You will need to provide basic information such as your names, address, date of birth, email address, and so on. You will also be required to provide a handle or Instagram username. This is the name that will identify you on Instagram. It is unique to you so that there is no confusion.

Post photos and videos

71

As soon as you provide the basic information required, you will need to verify your account via your email address. Posting is really easy. All you will need to do is to click on the posting icon and then select the video or photo you would like to post. Remember to select high quality, memorable, impressive, colorful images, and videos that will tell your story or showcase your brand.

Why Choose Instagram Marketing

Instagram is probably the social network that provides the most ideal platform for businesses. When it works, then it works really well. While the success rates will generally vary across the board, most businesses experience a much better return compared to most other social media platforms.

To be successful on Instagram as an entrepreneur, then your product should be tangible with visual properties such as colorful and presentable. This way, you can take professional shots of the product from different angles and then share them with your followers and also post them in your campaign ads.

Your product should also be geared towards young consumers, millennials, men and women, as well and international customers. If your product provides this, then you are on your way to success with Instagram marketing.

Instagram marketing information

The average engagement for ads and posts stands at 3.3% for major brands compared to only 0.07% on Twitter. Also, Instagram users are 25% more likely to be successful and wealthy which means they increase your chances of success. Also, almost over 20% of all web users have an Instagram account.

Success with Instagram marketing

Instagram is totally different from all other social media websites. Therefore, if you were successful on other social networks like Facebook, you will want to look at Instagram afresh. Even then, while it is slightly different from other social networks, the basics of getting your campaigns still apply.

The first thing you'll have to do is to take a closer look at what your target audience are responding to. What kind of topics, images, and videos do they seem to like and share? Also, check out what other brands are posting. Are they sharing funny videos or serious marketing messages? Learn what works for them and what does not. From here you will learn a lot about Instagram marketing and what approach is best.

Tips for success with Instagram marketing

Outsource the marketing aspect: Social media marketing can be quite time consuming and involving. If you are very busy with your business or other engagements elsewhere, then you should consider outsourcing the marketing process to a third party. There are plenty of digital marketers and marketing firms out there that can handle the process for you. You can still get involved in the marketing strategy and ad campaign creation. You can also monitor the progress, performance, and outcome of your campaigns.

Consider the financial resources needed: You will need to consider the financial aspect of posting ads on Instagram. When it comes to budgeting for the marketing campaign, you should consider the cost of hiring an ad firm as well as how long you want your campaign to run and so on.

Time is also a factor: Social media marketing takes time before the benefits or effects are noticeable. Therefore, do not spend all your time coming up with marketing strategies and things of that nature. If you are more focused on the intricacies of your business, then hire someone to help with this aspect. You may also outsource the function to someone else as has already been discussed.

Creativity: As a brand marketing on such a powerful and crucial platform, you need to ensure that you are as creative as possible. This means coming up with top-notch, impactful, memorable, and catchy ads that will impact viewers and compel them to act like you want them to. With a great strategy and suitable software, especially video editing software, you can prepare high-quality videos that your audience and the general public will appreciate.

Benefits of Instagram marketing

1. Brand awareness: One of the benefits of Instagram marketing is that it helps promote your brand to millions of users. Keep in mind that over 20% of all internet users have an Instagram account, so the chances of your message being seen are very high.

2. Customer feedback: When you place ads and other forms of marketing campaigns on Instagram, you receive customer feedback. Customer feedback is crucial for brands and businesses. You get to learn first-hand what your customers think about your products and services. The benefit, in this case, is that you get to receive customer feedback almost instantly.

3. Relationship building: If you wish to build relationships with customers, followers, and others, then Instagram is the best platform for you. Here you can allow your brand to express its amazing properties and benefits to your viewers. Use photos, images, memes, and videos to express personality and reach out to even more consumers.

4. Increase your interests and sales: When your brand grows then sales will follow almost automatically. Customers basically love good quality products so if your brand displays quality and provides a service or addresses a need that consumers have, then they will definitely purchase from you.

5. Potential to attract a new demographic: Since Instagram is a public platform, your brand and products can be viewed by numerous users especially if you have a public page. If you wish to attract an additional demographic such as international buyers, then Instagram provides you with an excellent opportunity to achieve this.

Tips on uploading the best Instagram photo

Most of the photos that you will upload to your Instagram will either be domiciled on your device or online. When you choose a photo to upload on Instagram, it can be oriented as either a landscape or portrait position. Select a photo that you want and then make any adjustments you wish such as adjust color, switch orientation, zoom, add captions, and so on. When you feel the image looks just right, you may then post it.

Instagram allows you to upload a maximum of 10 images and videos at one go. Therefore, if you wish to upload multiple images, Instagram provides you with the opportunity to do so. There is an icon consisting of two envelopes. Simply click this icon in order to upload multiple images.

You can also upload images and then schedule the posting. This is an excellent feature because posting times are crucial. If you are busy with little time to spend on your Instagram account, simply use the scheduling posting tool provided. This way, you will have your images posted at the times and dates that you choose. If you think most of your viewers or customers log onto Instagram in the evenings, then schedule your photos to be posted in the evening for maximum effect.

Additional Instagram tips

1. Focus on custom audiences and preferred demographics: Instagram allows you to send your marketing messages to a select group of individuals. You can choose who receives your messages in order to improve effectiveness. The select audience could include customers you have interacted with in the past, individuals on your email list, or even an audience that you created based on preferred criteria.

2. Make irresistible offers: Instagram is a very visual platform, and users often spend time viewing different posts including images and videos. With the right kind of content and message, you can take advantage of the platform and attract customers to your platform.

3. Make use of lookalike audience: One advantage that Instagram has is that it can help you identify a similar audience to the one that you seek. Therefore, after marketing to your current audience, you can then find a very similar audience to market to. This is a very effective approach that will help increase your reach.

4. Make use of hashtags: One of the most powerful features on Instagram is the hashtag. This platform is really driven by hashtags so while others may not take them seriously, you really should. They have a powerful way of connecting niche audiences and sharing a message.

5. Make use of custom images: While Instagram is huge on photos and images, stock photos are not allowed so make use of custom images of real people.

Editing your photos

Photos also need to be edited in some instances. There are various tools provided for editing photos. Here are some of the things that you can do with your posts.

Write a caption: when you post media such as videos and photos, you should add a caption. A caption is almost like a title. It headlines the image and provides a brief description so that others can learn more about the images and understand what message you are putting out for your viewers.

You can add tags or tag users that you believe need to view your post. You can also tag influential people, social media influencers, and anyone else that you like. Users often have what is known as handle or username. Make use of these handles so that more people get to view your posts. Also, use hashtags whenever possible. A hashtag often refers to a topic that is popular and being discussed. Whenever people discuss a particular topic via a hashtag, then your image will appear through these conversations which help to increase your reach.

Add a location: Anytime that you post items on your social media, you should take the time to add your location. This can be very helpful because it means your posts will appear whenever anyone mentions your location.

Share posts across social media: It is now easier than ever to share your content with others on social media. You can share your content including images and videos not just with followers on Instagram but with others on other social networks such as Facebook and Twitter. This greatly increases your reach and provides more opportunities for your brand and products.

Chapter 6: Marketing and Selling Online

YouTube Marketing

Did you know that YouTube is one of the largest and most popular search engines in the world? Yes, YouTube is second only to Google which is the world's largest search engine. Millions of users log in to YouTube each day to search for information, news, funny stories, entertaining content, and so much more.

Businesses, both big and small, have increasingly been using YouTube for their marketing purposes. Since numerous users are on this social networking site, it makes sense to post ads and marketing campaigns on the platform. Chances are that your potential customers are on the platform as well. If you can place targeted messages aimed at a certain demographic, then you will increase your chances of increasing your reach, gaining more followers, creating brand awareness, and acquiring new customers.

YouTube is the second most popular website

According to Alexa.com, a platform that ranks websites based on visitor numbers, YouTube is the world's second most popular website. While most people don't think of it as a search engine, more searches are conducted here than most other search engines. It enjoys visits from more than a billion active users and is available in over 76 different languages. Also, 33% of the time people spend online is used to watch videos.

Over 59% of business and company executives prefer to spend their time watching videos rather than read pages and pages of text. Also, more people in the age range between 18 – 49 access

YouTube than any mobile, cable, or broadcast network. Over 3.25 billion hours of videos are watched each month on YouTube. All this information shows that chances are very high that your customers, both current and future, are on YouTube.

YouTube is an excellent marketing platform. It allows users to create content and present it on the platform for viewers to enjoy and share. As a business owner and marketer, you can capitalize on YouTube to improve your brand presence and SEO ranking. As a business owner and entrepreneur, it is crucial to learn how to create great marketing content and videos then posting these on YouTube.

Create a YouTube channel

The first step in marketing on YouTube is to create a YouTube channel. However, maintaining a highly effective and good quality channel is not easy. It takes a lot of time to build up one because high-quality videos are costly to produce. On all social media sites, people post all other kinds of content. However, on YouTube, you can only post video content. Channels are created for uploading and hosting lots of content, so if you plan to upload just one video, then there is no need to create a channel.

Creating YouTube videos requires that you take to plan, strategize, make considerations, create videos, edit, and then market and analyze the performance. You should come up with plans and goals for your content and then use available tools to analyze the performance. The reason why you need to analyze how your videos perform is to understand what your viewers and customers think, what they are saying, and the tactics that are effective.

1. Create an account

Your first step even before grabbing your video camera is to create an account. This is not very simple because YouTube is owned by Google and as such you will need a Google account. As such, if you have a Gmail account, then you can easily start your own YouTube account and all other Google-affiliated accounts. It would, therefore, be easier to open your own Gmail account.

Once your Gmail account is verified and operation, you should then set up a YouTube brand account. At this stage, you are ready to upload content onto your YouTube account. However, before doing that, you should brand your account. Remember that you want to take advantage of the huge audience and massive viewership on YouTube. You will use your brand account to gain access to create an immense experience as well as editing permissions.

2. Sign in to YouTube

First, go to YouTube's homepage. This is at the URL www.youtube.com. Once on this page, you should confirm that you are logged in. Simply check at the top left-hand side corner of your YouTube page. If you are not logged, then you can do so from the same top-left corner. As soon as you log in, you will see a couple of buttons including "My Channel." Click on this button and create your channel. You can use your personal or business name.

It is advisable to use your brand name here because you really should be promoting your brand. Please note that you can always change your channel name should the need to do so arise. Therefore, do not worry too much about it as you can make changes from the settings page later.

3. Customize your channel

Now that you have your YouTube channel up and running, you should now customize it. Customization will help you to personalize it so that your followers, viewers and everyone else can recognize your channel and tell apart from all others. For starters, you will need to add an icon and some channel artwork. Anyone visiting your channel will see these first. Make them consistent and easy to remember. This way, any confusion with other channels will be eliminated, and your faithful customers, followers, and viewers will be able to identify you and find you easily. You channel icon is very similar to a profile photo on other social media. If you can keep this consistent, then you will fare really well in your social media marketing strategy.

Once these are set up, you should then provide your business details including address, company email, and channel description. You should also include direct links to your company website so any interested person can visit your website directly should they need to. You should also try and provide additional information about the content you are posting. For instance, are you posting videos about a particular topic or a variety of topics?

When creating videos for your channel, try and focus on showing your audience what the video is all about. Also, remember to request them to subscribe to your channel for more and better videos. A trailer that you prepare to whet your visitor's appetite will not be smothered by ads. This allows your audience to focus on your content before watching the entire video.

When you receive more than 100 subscribers, then your channel will become eligible for URL customization. However, to qualify, you will also need to have a channel art and an icon, and your channel should be at least 30 days old. Remember that you can assign other members of your team access to the account by adding their Gmail accounts. This way, they will be able to log onto the channel through their accounts and implement your marketing strategies or post videos.

Ideally, you can grant access to your channel at three different levels. These are the owner, manager, and communications manager. If you are the owner, you get to enjoy full editing rights over all your Google assets. You can remove or add managers as well as respond to comments, and alter business information. All the others have lesser roles in comparison and can be removed from the account at any time.

SEO optimization for your YouTube videos

Remember that YouTube is also a search engine. As such, you will need to optimize your videos in order to get them to rank on the first page of search results.

Creating high-quality videos for your channel is just half the work done. You will still need to optimize your videos. There are things that you can do so that your videos rank highly on both YouTube and Google.

Metadata

One of the most crucial steps in optimizing your videos is to focus on the Metadata. You need to create and optimize the metadata using appropriate keywords. Basically, metadata refers to information about your video that you put out there for your viewers. This information briefly lets users or viewers learn what the video is all about.

It includes video category, title, subtitles, tags, description, thumbnails and closed captions. When you create your metadata and provide the correct information, then YouTube will index it correctly and ensure that it appears in searches when people search for similar videos.

Title

Another important SEO aspect is optimization of your title. You need to optimize the description and title of your YouTube videos. People will always read the title of your YouTube video first. Therefore, ensure that it is compelling and clear. A good title is one that is catchy and will cause users to pause during a search and click on your video. Consider doing some keyword research for your videos. Also, ensure that your keywords are not longer than 60 characters, so they are not cut off in results pages.

Description

As you write your video description, you should focus on the first three lines because that is what YouTube will display after a search is conducted. If viewers want to read more than the first three lines, then they will need to click on the "Show More" tab. Therefore, include all important links as well as keywords at the initial stages of your description. Make sure you use essential or main keywords in order to optimize this aspect of your YouTube video.

You will also need to optimize your tags, category, and thumbnails in the same manner. If you follow these optimization tips and techniques, then you can trust that your video will rank highly on any YouTube search results based on your specific keywords.

YouTube videos

Once your videos are posted and you start receiving viewers, you should ensure that you remain honest and straightforward with your followers. As a business and even for individuals, providing credible information is crucial. This will ensure that you gain trust from your viewers. When you establish trust, then your followers will easily be converted to loyal paying customers.

After posting a video, your followers and other viewers are likely to comment on it. When they do, you should engage them rather than ignore them. Engaging your followers will ensure that they keep coming back and can be converted to leads.

Do not forget to link back your videos to your website. This way, if your customers love your content, trust you, and wish to know more about you, then you should make it easy for them to find your website. A simple link is in most cases sufficient.

Building Trust

Without regular interactions between brands and customers, some organizations would encounter immense marketing challenges. Platforms such as YouTube provide excellent opportunities for brands to engage with their customers and prospects. Such relationships help to build trust, and a community will form around your brand.

Make sure to publish honest content

As a business owner, you need to ensure that everything that you do is forthright and honest. Your followers, as well as the general public, will trust you when you are honest and forthright. This also means that you should publish honest content at all times.

This is content that comes from the heart. It does appeal to followers so make use of it.

Engage with your followers

Another crucial advice that you need to always apply is to engage your customers and followers directly. Social media is always a two-way street, so you need to ensure that you give as much as you take. You should, for instance, respond to comments, ask follow up questions and also like and leave comments on your followers' posts.

Put yourself out as an authority

YouTube users are very likely to follow you and trust you if they believe you are an authority in your niche. You become an authority when you provide excellent content about a niche continuously for a period of time. If you can answer your viewers' questions and address different topics, you will sooner or later be considered an authority in the field.

Focus on providing useful content

You also need to provide content that is helpful to your community of followers and viewers. A lot of people get onto social media seeking help, guidance, and advice. It is content producers like you that they look up to for assistance. If you can provide helpful content time and time again, then you will be able to gain the trust of your followers.

Increase traffic to your YouTube channel

It is impressive to note that over 500 million hours of YouTube videos are watched each day. The sad part is that less than 15% of business owners leverage on this viewership to promote their businesses. Fortunately, there are ways available to you to increase traffic to your YouTube channel.

Produce high-quality content

There is nothing that can increase your reach and attract viewers to your YouTube channel that killer content. If you want to engage an audience for hours and retain them for a long time, ensure that you routinely develop and deliver high value, informative, and entertaining content.

Optimize your YouTube videos

Even YouTube content needs to be optimized. Remember that YouTube is the world's second largest search engine. If you are able to competently optimize your content, then you can expect to attract more YouTube traffic to your website.

Use tools provided by YouTube to increase traffic

YouTube provides plenty of tools which you can use in order to optimize your content. For instance, you can use video editing software to help produce quality content. There is also a tool known as Tube Buddy which is designed to help with the management of smaller tasks. These tools will definitely boost your traffic.

Social Media Tips and Advice

Now that you have a presence in more social media websites, you need to have a proper approach in order to capitalize on the numerous marketing opportunities available. There is some etiquette that you will need to observe to increase your reach, attract more followers, promote your brands, attract more customers, and increase profits.

Engage with others

The first rule of thumb is that you should engage with followers and viewers. If you post content such as photos, videos, links to blogs, images and so on, then respond to all who leave comments. If a viewer asks questions, try, and answer the questions. If another leaves a positive comment, thank them and invite them to become a follower or subscriber.

Also, respond to anyone who shares or posts content. If your followers share content with them, make sure that you engage them in the most suitable manner. If they share content, then comment on the content and if they share a video then watch it and leave a positive comment. Some posts can be shared, and others liked. Engaging involves lots of different activity. The important thing is to be in regular communication with your followers. This will not only create a bond but will also enhance trust and draw them closer to you.

Give free value

Another crucial step that you need to keep in mind is to provide lots and lots of free value. This is crucial if you are to build trust. Find out what people within your industry are interested in or what problems bother them the most. When you can establish their problems and challenges, provide useful and practical solutions. Write blogs, provide images, research solutions, and get the best answers on each topic. Leave comments on blogs, websites, and different social media. When you do so, share a link to your blog where the solution can be found.

Keep doing this for a long time until people within your industry begin trusting you. You will need to do this for a period of six to nine months until trust is completely established and your authority on a subject matter is established. As you provide value and solutions, they will not only trust you but will view you as an industry leader, a guru, and expert in your field. It is only after you establish yourself that they will begin taking your advice and eventually start buying products or services from you.

How to provide free value

There are different ways of providing free value to viewers, followers, and social media users. You could provide free e-books full of relevant information within a certain niche. When you produce an e-book, make sure it is of very high quality. The content needs to be well written, claims should be backed up by facts, solutions to people's problems should be clearly defined, and any necessary media such as images, graphs, or links provided as well.

Remember to ask for email addresses when you provide the free e-books. Building an e-mail list of people within your niche is an excellent marketing strategy which you can later use when applying email marketing strategy.

Also, share blogs that you have written. Blogs provide an excellent platform for providing value and information. Share links to your blogs on social media and let others visit your blogs and read your content. Make sure you invite the readers to leave comments on your blogs and engage with them when they do. Also, collect emails of followers who come to your blog and engage with them. Just don't start pushing anything just yet until the time is right.

You can also provide stories and share real-life experiences. Users often love people who are real and who they can relate to. They normally dislike corporate types who are cold and are often too busy for their customers. So provide value most of the time but also share stories, posts, and all things that will add value to your readers.

Examples

You could begin your posts in a casual manner and say things such as, "Hey guys, here are 5 ways of solving that problem." Or you can perhaps say, "Here is something I tried that really worked." Then, share a link to the solution. Alternatively, you can invite all followers on one social media site to follow you on another site. Most people on Instagram also have a Facebook page so invite them from one platform to follow you on another platform and then follow them back.

Email Marketing

There are numerous marketing methods that you can use when you are an online entrepreneur. One of these is email marketing. For a while, you have been collecting e-mail when you shared value with your readers, followers, and general internet users.

There are various tools available to enable you to collect emails effectively and accurately. Once you have these emails, you should build a list. An email list provides you with an easy and effective way of contacting your readers. Remember that these readers are individuals within your industry who are interested in your posts and have gained value from your knowledge.

One of the best things that you can do with your online popularity is to collect as many email address from your viewers. You can then begin sending them emails telling them about important products that you have or any upcoming events. Let us say you have a business product launch or similar event, you should create high-quality emails and invite all your followers to the event.

Even as you send out these emails, try and offer an incentive. These incentives may include freebies, discounts, vouchers, and offers. Most consumers love discounted offers so do this to entice probably the first one hundred customers for instance. Email marketing is a very effective marketing strategy which can bring you success such as increased reach, engagements, more customers and increased profits.

Begin selling your products or providing services

Now that you have been giving for so long and providing a lot of value, it is time to begin taking. You do this by selling your products to your customers. At this stage, you should start advertising your products and brand and invite customers to your social media sites or websites where they can buy your products. If you applied your marketing strategy appropriately, then you should expect high sales with serious engagements across social media platforms and your website.

You can sell directly through your website or as an affiliate. There are numerous companies with high-quality products that offer affiliate products. Think about places such as Amazon Associates and Click Bank. These are established firms with successful affiliate marketing programs that are quite popular.

Affiliate marketing simply means selling on behalf of someone else. For instance, you can sell products within your industry but available on sites such as Amazon. If you provide high-quality information and present yourself as an expert, then your readers will trust you as an expert and will definitely buy products from you.

Remember that if you want to Affiliate Products, make sure you have tried the product itself and are 100% guaranteed that your audience are going to be happy with the product or service.

Best Places To Find Affiliate Products?

You can find affiliate products and services through websites such as:

- ClickBank
- Amazon Associates

- And emailing or messaging the business or business owner directly

Teach Others

By this stage, if you want, you are sufficiently experienced to teach, coach, mentor and train others. This is because you have pretty much acquired experience across all the stages of entrepreneurship. Teach interested persons about finding a niche, how to become an entrepreneur, how to start an online store, how to promote their brands and products, marketing across social media, optimization for search engines, and so much more.

You can teach by selling e-books or courses. There are sites that offer affiliate courses at a 50% commission. Teach whatever pleases you or has the greatest demand. At this stage, you can declare yourself an authority and expert in your niche so consumers and upcoming entrepreneurs will follow you and listen to your advice.

Conclusion

By now, you have learned a lot about how to become an entrepreneur and an expert in your industry. You have also learned how to become a successful marketer, an entrepreneur, and how to use social media sites for advertising and marketing purposes.

Building a brand may take time, but you will eventually get there. Do not take any shortcuts or disregard the information provided by experts. Remember that the internet is a global platform with billions of users. Therefore, if you build a strong brand and apply a great marketing strategy, then you can become as successful as you want and become a millionaire!

Finally if you found this book helpful, please leave a review on Amazon as it allows me to keep producing quality books.

www.ingramcontent.com/pod-product-compliance
Lightning Source LLC
Chambersburg PA
CBHW071501210326
41597CB00018B/2653